UNUSUAL AIRPLANES

UNUSUAL AIRPLANES

DON BERLINER

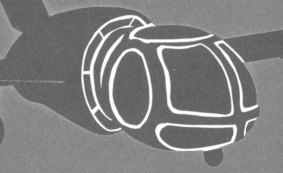

 Lerner Publications Company ▪ Minneapolis, Minnesota

ACKNOWLEDGMENTS: All of the photographs in this book have been provided by the author except for the following: pp. 8, 17, 24, 25, 38, Smithsonian Institution; p. 11, Northrop Corporation; p. 13, LTV Corporation; pp. 14, 18 (bottom), 23, NASA; p. 20, National Air and Space Museum; p. 21, Transavia; p. 22, Rockwell International; p. 28, Bell Helicopter Textron Company; p. 29, Edgley Aircraft Ltd.; p. 30, George Economos; p. 32, British Aerospace Corporation; p. 36 (top), Aerovironment; p. 4l, General Dynamics/Convair; p. 45, Sequoia Aircraft Company; p. 47, Hiroshi Seo.

LIBRARY OF CONGRESS CATALOGING-IN-PUBLICATION DATA

Berliner, Don.
    Unusual airplanes.

    (Superwheels & thrill sports)
    Summary: Describes a variety of airplanes invented through the years with unusual shapes and wing arrangements and run with human or solar power.
    1. Airplanes—Miscellanea—Juvenile literature. [1. Airplanes] I. Title. II. Series.
    TL547.B418   1986   629.133′34   85-24005
    ISBN 0-8225-0431-6 (lib. bdg.)

Manufactured in the United States of America

International Standard Book Number: 0-8225-0431-6
Library of Congress Catalog Card Number: 85-24005

  2 3 4 5 6 7 8 9 10 94 93 92 91 90 89 88 87

CONTENTS

INTRODUCTION **6**

UNUSUAL SHAPES **7**
   Unusual Wings *8*
   Unusual Tails *19*
   Unusual Fuselages *22*

UNUSUAL POWERPLANTS **27**
   Unusual Propellor Planes *27*
   Unusual Jet Planes *33*
   Other Unusual Power Sources *35*

SOME OTHER UNUSUAL AIRPLANES **39**
   The Largest and the Smallest *39*
   The Most and the Least Powerful *41*
   The Most Beautiful and the Ugliest *43*

CONCLUSION **47**

A close-up view of the 1903 Wright *Flyer*

The Wright *Flyer*, on display in Washington's National Air and Space Museum, has part of its tail in front (see page 5) and its propellors at the rear of the wing.

INTRODUCTION

For more than 80 years, men and women have been designing and building airplanes in an amazing variety of shapes and sizes. Even the very first airplane, the 1903 Wright *Flyer*, was pretty unusual with part of its tail in front and its twin propellors facing backwards. This book will look at some of the most unusual airplanes that have been built through the years. While many of these different-looking planes were not as successful as the more "tried-and-true" models, they often provided an idea or two that helped to make future airplanes better.

UNUSUAL SHAPES

All airplanes—from the smallest home-built model to the largest jet airliner—are composed of four main parts: wing, tail, fuselage, and engine. Although most planes have their parts in the "usual" places, at any airport, one can probably find several planes that are quite different. Some may have their wings in back and parts of their tails in front, and others might have one propellor in front and another in back. As the designing of airplanes became more scientific, designers began to realize that sometimes new shapes or a different arrangement of parts would work better in special situations.

In spite of their new shapes, all airplanes still flew in the same way. A wide surface, usually the wings, provided the lifting force, and the pilot's manipulation of the control surfaces on the wings and on the tail moved the plane to the right and to the left and up and down.

The Boeing 747 (see page 39) is the world's largest and most powerful passenger jet plane.

The Italian *Noviplano*, or "nine winger," was built in 1920. Although it was referred to as "the flying hotel," it never got off the ground.

UNUSUAL WINGS

For many years, almost all airplanes had two wings, one mounted above the other, and were called *"biplanes."* Then designers started to build *monoplanes* with just one wing and *triplanes* with three wings. Some even tried building planes with as many as three sets of triplane wings, but those experiments were not successful. After many years of constructing planes with the wings located in about the same place, designers today are again beginning to experiment with new shapes and positions for wings.

The Quickie sportplane (see page 10) is more efficient and safer to fly than planes with a more traditional shape.

Tandem Wing. Some new airplanes have tandem wings with one wing in front and the other in back. This type of plane can carry heavy and awkward loads of freight without becoming unbalanced. But the greatest advantage of the tandem-winged airplane is that it does not stall or spin when it is flown slowly.

The best-known tandem-wing airplanes are the small one-person Quickie and its big brother, the two-passenger Q2. These home-built sportplanes are made from carved blocks of plastic foam covered with thin layers of fiberglass cloth. Although the Quickie has only a 22-horsepower (h.p.) engine, it can cruise faster than 100 mph because it is so light and streamlined. The bigger Q2 has a 65-h.p. engine and can reach 200 mph.

The main wing of these small sportplanes is positioned just behind the cockpit, and there is a second wing near the airplane's nose. The front wing also serves as the horizontal part of the tail and has a moveable control surface along its trailing (rear) edge that acts as the airplane's elevator. Dozens of Quickies and Q2s are flying today, and hundreds more are being built.

Flying Wing. Some airplanes have no tails at all and practically no fuselages. Instead, they are almost entirely a wing. These "flying wings" use the whole airplane to provide *lifting force*, allowing them to carry a heavier load of people or freight than other airplanes of the same size. The first true flying wing was the single-seat experimental Northrop N-1M, which flew in 1940. It had no tail at all, and the pilot sat inside the wing.

Above: The N-1M's engines and pilot were located inside the wing. *Below*: The huge B-35 bomber had a 172-foot wing span and could travel for 10,000 miles without refueling.

The Northrop Corporation later built several larger, one-person N-9M flying wings, which performed well during their flight tests. Then in 1945, Northrop built the XP-79 flying-wing jet fighterplane. This fast plane also flew well, but it crashed on a test flight, and no more were built.

In 1946, the same company built several huge B-35 flying-wing bombers that had four 3,000-h.p. piston engines along the trailing edge of its broad wing. Although these strange-looking airplanes were able to carry a larger load farther and faster than any other bomber at the time, they were never put into full production. A year later, several B-35s were converted into jet-propelled B-49 bombers, which flew even faster. The U.S. Air Force still did not order them for its bomber squadrons, so all of the planes were finally withdrawn and broken up for scrap metal.

Today, there is a new interest in developing flying-wing airplanes because they are more efficient than standard planes. Delta-winged planes, with wings shaped like triangles, are quite similar to flying wings and are used as fighters, bombers, and supersonic transports. **Round Wing.** A variation of the flying wing is the circular wing, shaped like a flying saucer. In 1942, engineer Charlie Zimmerman believed that a round-wing airplane could fly fast but could also fly almost as slow as a helicopter when necessary. His employer, the Vought Corporation, built the experimental V-173, or "Flying Flapjack," with just such a wing.

Although the twin-engined test model was slow because of its small engines, it flew well and proved that Zimmerman's ideas had merit. As a result, the company decided to build the XF5U-1 "Flying Pancake" fighterplane for the U.S. Navy. That plane would

Although the "Flying Flapjack" could only fly about 100 mph, it was successful enough to be considered as a prototype for a U.S. Navy fighterplane.

have much larger engines and was supposed to be able to hover at 0 mph and fly as fast as 500 mph. Before it was finished, however, the project ran out of money, and the airplane was scrapped. At the time, right after the end of World War II, people were more interested in building jet fighters instead of propellor planes like the XF5U-l.

First flown in 1979, NASA's Ames/Dryden-1 (AD-1), is 40 feet long and weighs 2,000 pounds. During high-speed flights, its scissors wing can be pivoted at angles of up to 60 degrees for less drag and more efficient use of fuel.

Scissors Wing. Swept wings—wings that are slanted backward—are ideal for flying fast, but straight wings—wings that are perpendicular to the fuselage—are better for flying slowly. But if a plane has wings that can be set straight for slow speeds and then changed to swept-wings for high-speed flying, it will fly well at *both* fast and slow speeds. Several airplanes are able to change the angle of their wings in flight, and one of them is the U.S. Navy F-14 Tomcat.

The kind of variable-sweep wing used by the F-14 and other planes worked well, but it was heavy, and that cut down on the airplane's speed and maneuverability. Today, a new idea for variable-sweep wings, the "scissors" or "pivoting" wing, is being developed.

The scissors wing is set straight across for takeoffs and landings and for flying at slow speeds. Then, as the airplane increases speed, the pilot turns the wing to the diagonal so that one side is swept forward and the other side is swept back. The airplane looks completely out of balance, but it isn't.

The National Aeronautics and Space Administration (NASA) has tested a scissors-wing airplane and found that it flies quite well. NASA's AD-1 is actually a piloted scale model of a design for a supersonic airliner that may be built some day. It will be much lighter than airplanes that sweep both of their wings back, and it will not have the problem of becoming nose-heavy when the wings are swept toward the rear.

The first test flight of the Grumman X-29 research plane was on December 14, 1984, at Edwards Air Force Base in California.

Swept-forward Wing. An airplane with its wings swept back toward the tail has long been a symbol of high-speed flight. Such an airplane *looks* fast—and it *is*. Wings that are swept *forward* are also good for fast speeds. A big problem, however, is that swept-forward wings can twist and even break off when an airplane maneuvers sharply.

To prevent the possibility of their wings twisting off, the first airplanes with swept-forward wings were built especially for strength. But with the added weight, the advantages of their unusual wings were lost. Now, new materials called "composites" make it possible to build wings that are strong without being heavy.

The first airplane with lightweight, swept-forward wings was the Grumman X-29A research plane. The success of the Grumman test model could lead to more airplanes with swept-forward wings. Some day, planes with swept-back wings may actually look old-fashioned! **Channel Wing.** The channel wing is one of the most peculiar shapes for airplane wings. This wing has a large U-shaped section with a propellor just behind its trailing edge, which places a large area of the wing directly in front of the propellor. Even when the airplane is sitting still in mid-air, a great amount of air will be pulled over the wing, allowing the plane to lift itself off the ground without having to move very far forward.

W. H. Custer began working on channel wing airplanes in 1951 and built several different models. These planes fly like "normal" airplanes, but they can take off with almost no ground run, like a helicopter. Although Custer was never able to complete all of the tests he had wanted to make, his latest design is still being test flown.

A rare Custer channel wing. Located at the rear of the wing, the plane's propellors pulled the air over the U-shaped section of the wing, allowing the plane to take off almost straight up like a helicopter.

Above: One of the smallest canards is the home-built *VariEze*. *Below*: First flown in 1967, the B-70 *Valkyrie* supersonic bomber had six jet engines located beneath its wings.

UNUSUAL TAILS

Just like its wings, an airplane's tail can have varied shapes and be positioned in different spots on the plane. But whatever its shape and location, the tail's function is to help to stabilize the airplane by bringing it back to level flight after it has tipped or turned. The tail also carries some of the plane's control surfaces. The rudder on the upright part of the tail helps the airplane to turn right or left, and the elevator on the flat part of the tail helps it to go up and down.

Tail-first. Most airplanes have their tails located in the far rear of the fuselage to catch the blast of air from the propellor. But some of the most interesting airplanes have their tails in front. They are called "canards" because they look something like ducks. (*Canard* is the French work for duck.)

The first airplane ever built, the Wright brothers' 1903 *Flyer*, was built in the canard style. Orville and Wilbur Wright probably did not know exactly why they put the tail of their first airplane in front or why, a few years later, they built airplanes with the tails in back. Designers today, however, have learned that one reason for designing airplanes with the horizontal part of the tail in front and the vertical part in back with the rudder is safety.

Hundreds of canard airplanes are now flying, and two are the home-built Rutan *VariEze* and *Long-Ez*. These two-seat sportplanes are built of foam and fiberglass, making them both light in weight and strong. Because of their unique design, they are among the safest and most economical small planes in the world.

The largest canard airplanes ever built were two U.S. Air Force experimental supersonic bombers, the B-70 *Valkyrie*. Built in 1964, they had delta-shaped wings with canard surfaces in the nose and were meant to fly at 2,000 mph at an altitude of 80,000 feet. One of them crashed during an aerial photography mission, and the other was then withdrawn from service. Today it is on display at the U.S. Air Force Museum near Dayton, Ohio.

Tail-less. Some airplanes may look as if they have no tails, but their tails are actually combined with their wings. One such plane was the German Messerschmitt Me-163 *Comet*, the world's only rocket-powered fighterplane. Built near the end of World War II, the *Comet* flew at 600 mph, faster than any U.S. plane, and was used by the Germans to shoot down American bombers. The plane had numerous mechanical problems, however, and many blew up during landings.

The Me-163 had a standard vertical tail with a rudder but no horizontal tail. Instead, its elevator control surfaces were on the trailing edge of the wings. Because it did not have this bulky horizontal part, it was more streamlined and could fly faster, much like a flying-wing airplane.

Because they had not been tested carefully enough, more Messerschmitt Me-163 Comets were lost during landings than in combat.

The Australian Airtruk has two wings—and two tails.

Twin Tails. Many airplanes have twin vertical tails, one at each end of the horizontal tail. But an agricultural airplane built in Australia, the Airtruk, is the only plane with two complete tails. The tails are positioned far apart, one behind each wing, so they won't be damaged by the powerful chemicals that are sprayed out from the back of the central fuselage.

The Airtruk has a 300-h.p. engine, but it can cruise at only 120 mph. Its strong engine allows it to fly slowly at low altitudes while spraying out heavy loads of chemicals, seeds, or fertilizer. Under its main wing, the Airtruk has an extra short wing that stirs up the air and helps to scatter the chemicals or seeds over a wide area.

The P-82 Twin Mustang was one of the most efficient propellor-driven military planes ever built.

UNUSUAL FUSELAGES

The purpose of an airplane's fuselage is to hold the cockpit, the flight crew, and any passengers or freight. It also provides an attachment for the tail. In many airplanes, much of the back part of the fuselage is empty. Some planes, however, have unusual fuselages that are designed to avoid such wasted space.

Twin Fuselages. The North American P-51 Mustang was one of the best propellor-driven military airplanes ever built. When the U.S. Army's air force needed larger fighterplanes that could fly longer distances with heavier loads of guns and bombs, they decided to hook two P-51 fuselages together. This gave them an airplane with two pilots who could take turns flying on long missions. The plane would also have twice as much power and, therefore, would be able to carry more weight.

The double fuselage worked well, and the P-82 Twin Mustang performed exactly as its designers had hoped. Although the two pilots could talk to each other only by radio, each was able to fly the airplane alone. More than 250 Twin Mustangs were built, and they could fly at speeds up to 450 mph.

Lifting Body. The lifting-body airplane looks like it doesn't have any wings, but its thick, triangular fuselage acts as a wing under special conditions. This plane was designed to test the theory that a new kind of spacecraft without wings could operate while in orbit and then glide down through the air to a controlled landing. Several different versions of the Martin X-24 were tested. After being dropped from a huge B-52 Stratofortress bomber at high altitude, the X-24 test pilots took over to land the plane.

The X-24 worked so well that a similar delta-wing plane was used for the NASA Space Shuttle flights. After a powerful launch by a booster rocket, the wingless plane flew in space on its own power like any other spacecraft. Then its thick wings were used for support while it glided to a landing.

The success of the Martin X-24 test plane (*above*) led to the development of a similar plane for NASA Space Shuttle flights.

Inflatable. Imagine having an inflatable airplane that could be carried in the trunk of a car or in a small trailer and then blown up like a balloon when needed. The Goodyear Tire Company designed such a plane, the *Inflatoplane*. The deflated plane could be packed in a duffel bag and dropped by parachute to a pilot who had been shot down in combat. He would unwrap the plane and pump it up, start its small engine, and then fly the plane back to safety.

While the *Inflatoplane* was certainly an interesting plane, it wasn't very successful. It was flown many times by several different test pilots and flew fairly well, but its controls worked strangely because the airplane was flexible instead of being solid. When one of the control surfaces was moved, the airplane would twist slightly instead of rolling or turning.

Goodyear built two versions of the rubber airplane. One carried a single person, had a 44-h.p. engine, and cruised at 55 mph. The two-seater had a 65-h.p. engine and a cruising speed of 60 mph.

The Goodyear *Inflatoplane* was made of a rubberized fabric and was blown up with an air pump.

The only successful asymmetrical airplane ever produced, the BV-141

Asymmetrical. Even the oddest looking airplanes are *symmetrical*, or evenly balanced. If it has two wings on one side of the fuselage, it will have two identical wings on the other side. If there is an engine mounted on one wing, an identical engine will be in the same location on the other wing.

During World War II, however, the Germans built an observation aircraft, the BV-141, that did not even come close to looking balanced. Instead, it was *asymmetrical*, or unbalanced. The crew's compartment was stuck out on one wing to give the pilot and one observer a better view of the sky. Because the longer wing balanced the added weight of the cockpit on the shorter wing, the plane was not, in fact, as out of balance as it looked. Nevertheless, people called it the "Lop-Sided Lulu," and only a few were built because they looked so peculiar when they flew.

The shroud that covered the propellor of Jim Miller's fiberglass "Texas Gem" reduced the plane's noise and increased its power until high speeds were reached.

UNUSUAL POWERPLANTS

As already mentioned, most airplanes have either *piston* engines, which drive propellors, or *turbojet* engines. Some jet engines, called "turboprops," also drive propellors. While engines with propellors use less fuel than jets, jets have much more power. Although each engine has it own advantages and disadvantages, sometimes a modified or altogether different way of driving an airplane is needed.

UNUSUAL PROPELLOR PLANES

Shrouded Propellor. On an airplane that flies slower than 200 mph, a *shroud*, or covering, around the propellor increases the power and cuts down on the noise from the propellor. Jim Miller's "Texas Gem" Formula One racer has a shroud that fits very close to the whirling propellor. At first, it worked rather well and cut down on the noise enough to allow the pilot in the cockpit to talk with members of the ground crew just before takeoff. But as soon as the racer began moving faster than 200 mph, the advantages of the shroud were lost. The "Texas Gem" now races without any shroud.

Tilting Rotor. The movable rotor combines the advantages of airplane propellors with those of helicopter rotors. While a helicopter can take off and land vertically and hover in mid-air, it cannot fly much faster than 150 mph. And although an airplane can fly much faster than a helicopter, it needs a long runway for takeoffs and landings.

The experimental Bell XV-15 tilt-rotor craft can perform all of these maneuvers well. With its two rotors—one mounted on each wingtip—facing upward like those of a helicopter, it can take off vertically without a runway and

Above: When the Bell XV-15's rotor blades face forward like an airplane's propellors, it functions like a plane. *Below*: When its engines and rotors are turned upwards, the tilt-rotor convertiplane works like a helicopter.

fly like a helicopter. Then, when it rotors are tilted forward like airplane propellors, it can fly like an airplane.

The experimental XV-15 works so well that there is a great deal of interest in building larger models that could be used to carry passengers or, perhaps, to fly workers to off-shore oil drilling platforms. Tilt-rotor craft could make short trips more quickly than jet airliners because passengers could be taken directly to any destination rather than having to land at an airport.

The view from the clear, rounded cockpit of the ducted-fan *Optica* is truly panoramic.

Ducted Fan. Some aircraft are powered by a ducted propulsion unit, which is similar to a shrouded propellor. The engine and the propellor are completely inside the airplane, and they work somewhat like a jet engine. But more of the engine's horsepower can be converted into thrust because no air is lost from swirling over the propellor tips.

The buglike Edgley EA7 *Optica* is the newest ducted-fan airplane. Although it was designed especially for use in aerial photography, coastal patrol, and police work, no doubt many other uses will be found for this three-seater because the pilot and the observers can see so well from its unusual cockpit, which is shaped like an insect's eye and is almost totally clear. The *Optica* has a top speed of 125 mph and can fly as slow as 57 mph for up to 10 hours.

The Cessna *Skymaster* has two engines and two propellors—one of each on either end of its fuselage.

Push-Pull Propellor. Airplanes usually have two or more engines for more power and so they can keep on flying if one engine stops running. Most two-motored airplanes have one engine on the right wing and one on the left. If one of them stops, the airplane may become difficult to handle because all of the power will be applied from one side instead of from both, and the airplane will tend to fly sideways instead of straight ahead.

A solution to this problem has been push-pull propellors, which have one engine in the airplane's nose for pulling and the other in the tail for pushing. If one engine fails, the remaining engine will still be lined up with the center of the airplane, and the plane won't be pulled off to one side. This propellor arrangement also makes the airplane more streamlined because it will not have bulging engine compartments on each wing to create wind resistance.

One push-pull airplane is the Cessna *Sky-master*. It has a central fuselage for the pilot and passengers and an engine at either end. Two slim metal *booms*, or extensions, running back from behind the wings hold the tail in place.

An even more streamlined push-pull airplane is the experimental Rutan *Defiant*. Like many of Burt Rutan's designs, the *Defiant* is a canard with a thin swept-back wing at the rear and a small canard surface at the nose. It has a 160-hp engine at either end of the fuselage and can fly well with either engine.

The louvered openings on the sides of the Harrier VTOL jet fighterplane can be turned to provide vectored thrust, which allows the plane to fly forward or up and down like a helicopter.

UNUSUAL JET PLANES

Vectored-Thrust. By making use of *vectored thrust*, a jet airplane can be designed to fly like a helicopter. The powerful blast coming from the jet engine can be turned, or *vectored*, from straight back for normal flying to straight down for flying up and down.

The pilot activates vectored thrust with a lever that turns the end of the engine's exhaust pipe while the rest of the engine remains fixed in place. A vectored-thrust jet can blast itself straight up without having to roar down a runway for a mile or more before getting off the ground.

Once in the air, the pilot can turn the exhaust pipe to point straight back, and the airplane will move forward like any other jet. To land the plane vertically like a helicopter, the pilot turns the exhaust downward again and controls the throttle very carefully. The plane can then set straight down on a landing pad no larger than a baseball diamond.

The most famous and successful airplane that uses vectored thrust is the British Aerospace Harrrier. In service since 1969 with the British Royal Air Force and since 1971 with the U.S. Marine Corps, the Harrier looks like a regular jet fighter except for the unusual jet pipes on its sides just below the wings. These pipes can be swiveled by the pilot to provide vectored thrust.

The Harrier can fly at speeds from 740 mph to 0 mph. It can sit in mid-air without moving and can then slowly back up or fly sideways. When it is flying forward at high speed, its jet pipes can be turned slightly downward and back again. This allows it to be maneuvered more sharply than any other type of jet fighter.

To date, vectored-thrust airplanes are used only by the military for landing and taking off from beaches or clearings in a jungle and to attack enemy positions with guns, bombs, and rockets. In the future, it is possible that larger vectored-thrust airplanes may also be used for carrying passengers and freight.

The Dornier Do31 uses its jet engines for forward flight and its separate wingtip-mounted engines for lifting off the ground.

Direct Lift. Another type of VTOL (Vertical Take-Off and Landing) jet has regular jet engines to drive it forward and separate smaller engines for use during takeoff and landing. The German Dornier Do31 has its small vertical-flight engines mounted in pods at the wingtips. Doors close over these vectored-thrust engines, making them more streamlined when the airplane is flying forward.

Only one Do31 was built for test flying. It flew fairly well, but the small engines at the wingtips were only useless, extra weight when the plane was flying forward. This was such a waste that no more Do31s have been built.

OTHER UNUSUAL POWER SOURCES

Human Power. Humans have always dreamed of flying like birds. Even before the Wright brothers' successful flight in 1903, others were trying to build flying machines consisting of birdlike wings attached to the pilot's arms and legs. Although that idea has never worked, people have never given up trying to find a way to fly without the help of an outside power source.

In 1959, Henry Kremer of Great Britain offered a prize to the first person who could fly around a figure-8 course using nothing but muscle power. Many groups of student-engineers built airplanes that were propelled by human "pedal power." While some of these craft could fly a mile or more in a straight line, they were difficult to turn because they flew so slowly—at 10 mph or less.

Finally in 1976, designer Dr. Paul Mac-Cready developed his first *Gossamer Condor*. Built from thin aluminum tubing and balsa wood and covered with Mylar, a very thin plastic sheeting, the *Condor* had a wingspan of 96 feet. Yet, without its "engine," racing bicyclist Bryan Allen, it weighed only 70 pounds. In 1977, Allen flew the *Condor* around a one-mile figure-8 course in California in 6½ minutes to win the Kremer Prize of 50,000 British pounds (about $100,000).

Kremer next offered a much larger prize of 100,000 pounds (about $200,000) for the first human-powered flight across the English Channel between England and France. This flight presented a much greater challenge because it would mean crossing 22 miles of open water in an area known for severe weather instead of traveling over California's peaceful Mohave Desert.

Above: The original human-powered *Gossamer Condor* in flight. *Below*: This second *Gossamer Albatross* is identical to the first model that successfully crossed the English Channel in 1979.

Three new *Gossamer Albatross* were built for the Channel flight. In 1979, Bryan Allen took off from the English coast and pedaled hard for 2½ hours to reach his destination, totally exhausted. He had traveled at speeds of 12 to 15 mph and at altitudes ranging from 25 feet to 6 inches above the water.

The Gossamer airplanes were true human-powered flying craft. But flying them is such strenuous work that not many more may be built. It is much easier to attach a small engine to one of these airplanes and let the pilot sit back and enjoy the flight!

Solar Power. Another dream of many has been to be able to take off and fly with an engine that doesn't use a traditional fuel source. By 1980, advances in the development of solar cells that could convert sunlight into electricity led people to think seriously about a solar-powered airplane.

Once again, Dr. Paul MacCready was the first to develop this new kind of aircraft. In late 1980, his *Solar Challenger* flew for the first time, with pilot Janice Brown making 50-mile trips in two hours.

Almost the entire surface of the *Challenger's* wings and horizontal tail was covered with shiny, expensive solar cells. Each cell converted a small amount of sunlight into electricity, which, like the piston engine of a standard airplanes, turned a propellor.

After the *Challenger* had been tested and improved, it was able to fly up to eight hours at heights of 14,000 feet (more than 2½ miles). As long as it traveled in sunlight, its solar cells could produce enough electricity to turn the propellor. But the cells could not perform well when the sun was blocked by a cloud. In 1981, the *Challenger* was flown from Paris to London in 5½ hours at an average speed of 30 mph.

Human- and solar-powered airplanes have been remarkable achievements in the history of aviation. Although these planes were successful, their future probably lies more in competing as sportplanes than as being used as commercial planes.

The "Spruce Goose," the largest airplane ever built, flew only once.

SOME OTHER UNUSUAL AIRPLANES

In addition to having unusual wing, tail, or fuselage arrangements or being powered by some uncommon fuel source, a number of airplanes have been called "unusual" because of some remarkable feature such as their size or their general appearance. From among the more than 10,000 different kinds of airplanes that have been built since 1903, here are some that will be especially remembered.

LARGEST AND SMALLEST

The Largest. The largest airplane that is most often seen is the Boeing 747 wide-bodied "jumbo jet." When carrying 50,000 gallons of jet fuel and more that 400 passengers, it weighs 800,000 pounds or more. Several hundred 747s are flown by airlines around the world. In the same period of time, one 747 airliner can carry more people across the Atlantic Ocean than the largest ocean liner because the 747 can make several trips back and forth while the ship is steaming along on its initial journey.

The U.S. Air Force Lockheed C-5A Galaxy transport plane is about the same size as a 747. The C-5A can carry more than 200,000 pounds of freight, such as 16 small trucks, at one time. The plane's wings stretch 223 feet from tip to tip, and it is 248 feet in length.

Better known as the "Spruce Goose" because it was made mainly of wood, the Hughes HK-l Hercules was the largest airplane ever built. It had a wingspan of 319 feet, 11 inches (similar to a football field), and its total wing area was 11,430 square feet—more than one-fourth acre! The HK-1 was designed to carry 700 fully equipped soldiers.

Despite its size, the tiny *CriCri* sportplane is strong, easy to maneuver, and a pleasure to fly.

The HK-1 was designed by Howard Hughes, a well-known movie producer and speed-record pilot. Hughes believed his seaplane could play an important role in World War II by carrying men and supplies across the oceans and evading the German and Japanese submarines that were sinking so many U.S. cargo ships. But the first HK-1, built at a cost of 40 million dollars, was not completed until after the war, and it made only one short test flight in 1947. Today, it is on display in Long Beach, California.

The Smallest. The smallest true airplane that has flown is the *CriCri*, or *Cricket*, a homebuilt sportplane. Designed by Michel Colomban, a French engineer, in 1973, the all-metal, single-seat *CriCri* weighs only 155 pounds when empty. Its wingspan is only 16 feet with an area of 33 square feet, which is less than a 5- by 7-foot rug.

The Convair B-36 superbomber is powered by six rear-propellor "pusher" piston engines and four jet engines.

Even though the *CriCri* looks like a toy, it is a strong and nimble airplane that can be flown safely through difficult aerobatic maneuvers. Powered by two 15-h.p. snowmobile engines, it can cruise at 118 mph. Hundreds are now being built in workshops all across the United States.

MOST AND LEAST POWERFUL

The Most Powerful. Although airplanes with piston engines and propellers are not as powerful as jet airplanes, some are still quite powerful. The most powerful piston-engined airplane ever built was the Convair B-36 super-

Although the Bede BD-5 can travel as fast as 275 mph, it cannot travel very far or carry a heavy load.

bomber. Built in the 1950s, the plane had six 28-cylinder, 3,800-h.p. engines as well as four jet engines that each provided 5,200 pounds of thrust. A B-36 could carry a load of bombs weighing 10,000 pounds for 10,000 miles without refueling.

Airplanes with jet engines can fly much faster and much higher than those with propellors. The most powerful jet airplane that has flown so far is also the largest—the Boeing 747. The 747 has four huge engines, each producing more than 50,000 pounds of thrust. It can carry hundreds of passengers for many thousand miles at 600 mph.

The Least Powerful. Probably the least powerful piston-engined airplane is the home-built Croses EAC-3 *Pouplume*, or "Flea Feather." This tiny one-person French sportplane has a 10½-h.p. motorcycle engine and cruises at 31 mph. The *Pouplume* can take off on a 200-foot runway and can land with a ground roll of only 80 feet.

The least powerful jet-propelled airplane ever built is the Bede BD-5J. Used primarily for sport flying and demonstrations at air shows, the all-metal single-seater weighs only 450 pounds when empty. Although its single engine can build only 200 pounds of thrust, it can still fly at 275 mph. Since a limited number of BD-5Js were constructed, they are usually seen only at air shows or fly-ins.

MOST BEAUTIFUL AND UGLIEST

The Most Beautiful. Although not everyone will agree on which airplanes should be called "beautiful," there are a few planes that most people recognize as being very special looking. One such plane is the Supermarine Spitfire. Built in England during World War II, the Spitfire was one of the most important military airplanes of all time.

The Spitfire had a gracefully tapered elliptical wing, a long, shapely nose, and a trim, rounded tail, and it was powered by a Rolls Royce V-l2 engine. Everyone would stop and watch when it swept across the sky. Today, there are only a few Spitfires still flying, and they are only displayed on special occasions.

Many flying enthusiasts consider the Supermarine Spitfire a truly beautiful airplane. The Spitfire weighed 3,000 pounds and was 30 feet long with a 37-foot wing span. It could travel at 350 mph.

The graceful lines of the Falco F.8L make it a lovely plane. With a 20-foot wing span, the 21-foot Falco has a 160-h.p. engine and can fly at 200 mph.

Another truly good-looking airplane is the Falco F.8L. This Italian factory-built sport-plane was designed in 1956 by Ing Stelio Frati, a person who knew that if an airplane looks great, it will probably fly well, too. The Falco first became popular with wealthy European sport enthusiasts. Later it was available as an American home-built plane that any aviation buff could build.

The Ugliest. If there are beautiful airplanes, there must be some especially odd-looking ones, too. This does not necessarily mean that they don't fly well, only that they look worse than most.

The Fairey *Gannet* is one such plane. It has bulges and lumps, and its wings fold twice, making it look like everything is broken. Because the Fairey *Gannet* was used for many

The wings of the Fairey *Gannet* fold so the plane wouldn't take up so much space inside an aircraft carrier. The 43-foot *Gannet* had a wing span of 54 feet and weighed 22,500 pounds. With a 3,000-h.p. engine, it traveled at 300 mph.

years by the British to search the ocean for enemy submarines, it was equipped with a great deal of special radar and other equipment that stuck out to spoil its shape.

CONCLUSION

Clearly, the first 80 years of aviation were filled with some truly unique airplanes. Although some never got beyond the first test model because they didn't fly as well as existing airplanes, each new design played a part in the development of the airliners, private planes, sportplanes, and military planes that we know today.

Future airplanes are expected to be even *more* unusual. And because of the greater variety of materials available for their construction, many of them will fly better and more efficiently than the planes of today.

One of the fattest propellor-driven airplanes, the Gee-Bee Z or "Flying Milk Bottle," could be called either a not-so-good-looking plane—or one of the cutest! This is a reproduction of the 1931 racer. Only 15 feet, 1 inch in length, it weighed 2,280 pounds and could fly as fast as 270 mph. Its cockpit was in the back to balance the heavy 700-h.p. engine in the front.

Superwheels & Thrill Sports

Airplanes
  AEROBATICS
  AIRPLANE RACING
  FLYING-MODEL AIRPLANES
  HELICOPTERS
  HOME-BUILT AIRPLANES
  PERSONAL AIRPLANES
  RECORD-BREAKING AIRPLANES
  SCALE-MODEL AIRPLANES
  YESTERDAY'S AIRPLANES
  UNUSUAL AIRPLANES

Automobiles & Auto Racing
  AMERICAN RACE CAR DRIVERS
  THE DAYTONA 500
  DRAG RACING
  ICE RACING
  THE INDIANAPOLIS 500
  INTERNATIONAL RACE CAR DRIVERS
  LAND SPEED RECORD BREAKERS
  RACING YESTERDAY'S CARS
  RALLYING
  ROAD RACING
  TRACK RACING

  CLASSIC SPORTS CARS
  CUSTOM CARS
  DINOSAUR CARS: LATE GREAT CARS
    FROM 1945 TO 1966

  FABULOUS CARS OF THE 1920s & 1930s
  KIT CARS: CARS YOU CAN BUILD YOURSELF
  MODEL CARS
  RESTORING YESTERDAY'S CARS
  VANS: THE PERSONALITY VEHICLES
  YESTERDAY'S CARS

Bicycles
  BICYCLE MOTOCROSS RACING
  BICYCLE ROAD RACING
  BICYCLE TRACK RACING
  BICYCLES ON PARADE

Motorcycles
  GRAND NATIONAL CHAMPIONSHIP RACES
  MOPEDS: THE GO-EVERYWHERE BIKES
  MOTOCROSS MOTORCYCLE RACING
  MOTORCYCLE RACING
  MOTORCYCLES ON THE MOVE
  THE WORLD'S BIGGEST MOTORCYCLE RACE:
    THE DAYTONA 200

Other Specialties
  BALLOONING
  KARTING
  MOUNTAIN CLIMBING
  RIVER THRILL SPORTS
  SAILBOAT RACING
  SOARING
  SPORT DIVING
  SKYDIVING
  SNOWMOBILE RACING
  YESTERDAY'S FIRE ENGINES
  YESTERDAY'S TRAINS
  YESTERDAY'S TRUCKS

Lerner Publications Company
241 First Avenue North, Minneapolis, Minnesota 55401